Hell in my Head

how a family coped with stress and
trauma following military conflict

John F. Bennett

Hell in my Head

Published by The Conrad Press in the United Kingdom 2020

Tel: +44(0)1227 472 874
www.theconradpress.com
info@theconradpress.com

ISBN 978-1-913567-31-6

Typesetting and Cover Design by:
Charlotte Mouncey, www.bookstyle.co.uk

The Conrad Press logo was designed by Maria Priestley.

Printed and bound in Great Britain by Clays Ltd, Elcograf S.p.A.

Contents

Foreword

I feel deeply honoured to write the foreword for this moving book about the issues faced by members of the Armed Forces community.

The book takes you back in time, where you can start to visualise some of the traumas and then see their long-term impact on the individuals and in turn on the various families. It demonstrates through these personal stories and excellent story telling how things are changing in the understanding and support available to individuals.

What strikes me is how some things really don't change. One of those is the impact on the family, which is often not recognised. I hope through reading this excellent book those of us who have not served will have a greater compassion and understanding for those who have served and in turn their families.

For those from the Armed Forces community, this book gives a greater insight into the wider range of mental illness that can affect those who have served, for example Adjustment Disorder.

There are now many more services available that you, your friends, family and colleagues can access including mental health support. There is much to be learnt from this book but the main one is please do ask for help if you need it.

Kate Parkin (DCR (T) BSc MBa DMS)
NHS Director Armed Forces Network
www.sussexarmedforcesnetwork.nhs.uk

Dedicated to all those who went before

Introduction

I was born into a rural working-class family in 1957 in the Kentish hamlet of Bramling, part of the parish of Ickham in East Kent.

Most of my grandparents, uncles, aunts and cousins were living within an easy walk of my childhood home. Being born twelve years after the end of World War II the adult conversation and anecdotes were mainly from that period.

Of course, for most people of that generation, the war was the most 'exciting' period of their lives. With the fear and uncertainty of not knowing how the war was affecting them on the home front, or relatives away in far flung parts of the world. The parents and grandparents of this era had gone through this upheaval within living memory, some for a second time.

Unlike the world of today where the internet brings us up to date at the touch of a key. Live information on world events is plastered across the television as it happens. The only information back then was censored newspapers and carefully scripted and conservative information, released in broadcasts for the few people who owned a new fangled radio.

Music during this era was primarily the 1940s big band music my parents enjoyed during their earlier years, interspersed with 1950s romantic ballads by the likes of Doris Day and Guy Mitchell. Rock and Roll had not permeated into our household.

The preparation for Sunday lunch times was always to the tunes of *Three-Way Family Favourites* on the Light programme broadcast simultaneously on medium wave from London, Germany and Hong Kong with Cliff Michelmore and his wife Jean Metcalfe. The household interest in all thing's military was abound with constant reminiscing and storytelling.

Stories about the exploits of parents, uncles and great uncles would abound at family gatherings but one name was never mentioned in public. The curiosity of a youngster would eventually ask about my mother's eldest brother and the room fell silent. Grandfather would get up and disappear for hours and everyone would speak in hushed voices thereafter.

My memories of my grandparents are vivid. My father's parents were quite different to my mother's. Grandad Bennett was a softly-spoken man with a broad Kentish accent who worked for HW Mount on a fruit farm in Littlebourne, near Canterbury in Kent. After he retired, he became the village postman for many years until ill health curtailed his ability to work.

Nanny Bennett looked after my father's disabled sister who went everywhere with her as if she was her shadow.

Nan always looked tired and worn out but sheer determination drove her out of bed every morning. They lived in Ickham in one of the new post-war council houses. Grandad was a keen gardener and always had a productive vegetable garden.

My mother's parents were different; their home was full of chipped furniture, damaged ornaments and mismatched cutlery. I found out many years later these were salvaged items from their collapsed antique shop which I will discuss in a later chapter.

Grandad Garrett was a quiet withdrawn man who sat in his chair by the fire but whenever I visited, he would often stare at me and sometimes appear to cry before walking out of the room.

He was prone to playing the old upright piano with some dexterity given the arthritis in his joints. He would play the World War 1 classics with gusto, but on close inspection the tears would be running down his face. He looked so sad all the time. I don't remember him working but he hit retirement age when I was very young.

Nanny Garrett was a bright cheerful lady, a little wizened in her senior years but lively and full of fun. I spent quite a bit of time with her when I was a small child while my parents were working.

I want to investigate the lives of some of the family members and draw comparisons of how their mental illnesses would have been dealt with during the current era, with the advances of medicine and its more recent breakthroughs.

The journey to completion has been a hard one, the exploits of the WW1 generation told through relatives needed to be verified with the regimental records and through the census data and has been somewhat of a roller coaster.

The information from family members became muddled and Edwin's, Edward's, Charlie's and John's became a confused family tree. I still find it so incredible that our family were so lucky to have all four brothers return home.

I experienced some problems when I returned home from operations which I had to overcome myself in 2001/2002, the problems of veterans' mental health were not given priority or indeed, even recognised until very recently.

Whilst working with the Army regimental association over the last few years the seed of an idea came to me. I have been dealing with ex soldiers suffering various degrees of PTSD and depression through conflicts in Iraq, Afghanistan and to some degree the Northern Ireland veterans.

Researching the family history, it was blatantly obvious that I had a story to tell which must mirror other families' experiences of this terrible illness. I have attended several Mental Health courses recently to give me the insight to write this book and to help members of my regiment overcome this debilitating illness, and now I am a Mental Health qualified first aider working with the regimental association.

Mental illness has been a focus in our lives over the years. My stepson had an episode of psychosis just a few years ago which as a family, we had to deal with at first hand. Sadly, the mental health services in London were overstretched and creaking at the seams. He was discharged into our care as a statistic with very little help.

The next eighteen months were a rollercoaster, with us having to think on our feet and badgering the system to get help and support with no training whatsoever.

Chapter 1

Frederick Charles Garrett, 1893-1972

The early years

Frederick (Fred) Garrett was born in Folkestone in 1893. His parents were Charles Winter Garrett, a notable footballer, who played for Folkestone town during their heyday period of the late 1800s and early 1900s, and Alice Garrett nee Johnson. The family lived at 7 North Street, Folkestone for most of Fred's early years. Fred was a keen sportsman and particularly enjoyed playing football.

The Johnson family were quite wealthy for the period, owning many properties in Folkestone and were connected to many mayors and local dignitaries in the local area. Their main business was a thriving antique shop at 37 High Street, which was hugely popular. Susan Johnson, Fred's grandmother was widowed during the early 1900s and continued the family businesses on her own.

When Fred attained the age of fourteen, he went into the family business, moving in with his grandmother, living above the shop where he trained in the antique business. He also learned about property maintenance and developed a financial acumen whilst still engaging in his passion of football!

In 1911 Fred was playing in a match at home when he was spotted by a talent scout from Arsenal football club. Fred was invited to go for a trial where he played well and was offered a contract to play on a semi-professional basis.

Back then if you were selected to play you had to make your own way to games, depending where the match was. The team selection would be relevant to where guys lived, for instance if Arsenal played in Luton then it would be extremely unlikely that someone living in Folkestone would have been chosen for the match, more likely the team would come from players living in London or more to the north. No hotels or overnight stays during the early days of football!

In 1914 the prospect of war loomed and some stark choices needed to be made for the twenty-one-year-old Fred Garrett. Should he give up the family business, which undoubtedly would have folded as his grandmother was becoming very ill and frail?

Susan passed away later in the year and Fred was left the family business and all the property in Folkestone. This provided a further dilemma, should he give up his passion for the opportunities that football had given him? However, the national fervour and peer pressure would eventually prevail.

Ultimately Fred joined the Folkestone troop of the Kent

Cyclists battalion which was classified as a home defence unit part of the territorial force.

As Fred was deemed unable to be mobilised for service abroad, he spent his weekends when not playing football, with the territorial unit exercising in the local area.

In October 1915 the decision to join full time was taken away from Fred. he had maintained the business which had saved him from compulsory mobilisation, but one night Zeppelin L14 dropped bombs on the Otterpool army camp where Folkestone racecourse now stands. Unfortunately a stray bomb was dropped on the town.

This bomb landed in the yard behind the shop at 37 High Street but didn't completely explode, the force of the blast and shock wave brought down the interior of the three story building. It collapsed like a pack of cards.

Luckily Fred was visiting his family in North Street and arrived home to be greeted with nowhere to live and the lucrative family business a pile of rubble. The following day they salvaged whatever could be saved but this amounted to very little.

After the clean up Fred decided to join up full time and he transferred into the local regiment the Queens Own Royal West Kent's. Fred joined the 11th (Lewisham) battalion which needed replacements due to huge losses sustained in many of their initial actions of the war.

It is interesting that some distant relatives petitioned the government to have Fred released to return to Folkestone. There were some loose ends requiring his attention primarily to close down the business that he as the only antiques expert, had to undertake. It seems that they wanted a share out of the proceeds of the remaining stock. Another pressure to contend with for the young Fred.

Fortunately, the relatives had to wait until the end of the war as the petition failed. It's interesting that the petition carried the signature of the Chief Constable of Kent to give weight to the application. Fred soldiered on and to add further complications to his life he received a letter from the solicitors of his grandmother.

This stated that some more distant relatives were challenging the will because they felt they had a call on the estate. Fred would have been unable to get special leave to return to Folkestone to resolve the issue. Eventually this was concluded and Fred retained the estate after many hundreds of pounds in solicitors' fees.

After a period of refresher training at Shorncliffe barracks in Folkestone, Fred went to France with a group of reinforcements for the 11th Battalion.

The group of soldiers would have marched with all their kit from Shorncliffe camp, (probably the tented complex at Dibgate, just beyond St Martins Plain training camp), through the town to the Leas, finally down what is now known as the Avenue of Remembrance to the harbour below.

They would then have boarded the ship to France. This, during those far-away years, would have been a daily occurrence with thousands of units and reinforcements travelling down that same route. Faces would be smiling, full of hope and national pride, all along the route people would gather and cheer and call out, it would have been unlikely that those innocent youngsters would realise what lay in store.

Fred Garrett's abilities as a footballer would have been known on his enlistment but this didn't work in his favour. Fred was always taken out of his unit to play football matches for the army back in the UK.

Sadly, this did him no favours as just as he bonded with his comrades they would be left to go on an assault or operation without him, then when Fred returned, he would be greeted by reinforcements with hardly any of his previous friends still there.

Over the next couple of years this continued, and together with a minor head wound (a random bullet went through his helmet, grazed his head and then ricocheted around the back exiting almost exactly opposite to the entry point) leaving him with recurring headaches for the rest of his life.

Fred also suffered minor chlorine gas effects from an exploding shell a few hundred yards away during the first gas attack of the war at Ypres. This needed treatment and would eventually curtail his football career.

When he returned to his unit, he was advised the battalion was about to disband, and he was posted to the 8th battalion. He was given the appointment of batman to Lieutenant Donald Dean which took him away from the normal day to day routine, interspersed with his forays back to the UK and other football matches at divisional locations within the rear areas. The effect of always going back to new faces eventually took its toll.

The fresh-faced individuals full of hope and fearlessness looked upon him as a someone who seemed to be away when the tough times happened. This was true but not through Fred's making.

Of course, this was not the case, Fred had seen his share of the action. In later years he would talk of Donald Dean with a great deal of fondness, I believe he was one of the few people who could see that playing football at a high level was a distinct disadvantage to his wellbeing and career.

Over the period of 24th to 26th September 1918 Fred was playing a match against the Royal Navy at Portsmouth. This coincided exactly with the defensive action led by Donald Dean near Lens, which would ultimately earn Lieutenant Dean the highest military order, the Victoria Cross.

Upon his return he felt a bit of a fraud, he had missed the biggest action his platoon had seen for a while and was treated like a new boy or a reinforcement. Again after a few weeks, he was posted first for a brief spell with the Labour corps, and then a battalion of the Lancashire fusiliers where he saw out the remaining time in uniform.

Fred Garrett had seen his fair share of the horrors of war during his service in France but because the continuity of front line service was broken, he felt cheated and, in many ways, believed he had let his mates down and of course felt let down by the system.

Fred applied for a football trial with the Heart of Midlothian football club in the last year of the war and they were quite keen to see him once his service had come to an end. It had become clear however, that as time went on the possibility of Fred ever playing again was diminishing.

The effects of the gas on his lungs reduced their capacity and as a striker he needed to be on top form. Fred saw his second career drifting away. The Fusiliers returned to Shorncliffe and awaited demobilisation but although he was only a couple of miles from home the battalion eventually was entrained to Preston, the home of the Lancashire fusiliers. Twenty four hours later he was back on a train to Folkestone.

After demobilisation Fred returned to Folkestone where he married his fiancé Rose Newing (more about the Newing's in chapters to follow).

The inter-war years

Fred and Rose faced a dilemma, the family business was gone and all that remained were the properties around the town and the small rent that they made.

They had to live somewhere so they rented a small flat whilst they made more permanent arrangements. Fred decided to sell all the properties at auction, which may not have been the most profitable way of selling them, but it would have made enough money to buy their own home quickly and set themselves up. Fred and Rose bought 67 Warren Road Folkestone in 1919, the family then soon grew with Aubrey being born in 1920, Fred (Bill) 1922, Gladys 1923 and finally Dennis in 1927.

Fred was grateful he had learnt about house maintenance whilst looking after the properties that the family owned. He worked for a local builder where he learnt the skill of carpentry and when needed, at their own undertakers' business as a pall bearer.

Over time he became unsettled. He had trouble with nightmares and sleeping became more difficult. Fred and many of the friends and colleagues had seen unspeakable things during their war service.

A man hardly ever discussed these things with his family. It just was not the 'done thing' It was only at the annual Royal

West Kent reunion they would talk about the unspeakable subject, aided by a good meal and copious amounts of beer. Fred was no different to his peer group, he had seen and done horrific things but having been brought back to England every couple of weeks had not helped his state of mind.

Everyone has a breaking point, one minute you have a thriving profitable business and a home and in an instant that was gone, a promising football career which after the gas attack was lost. The final straw was the death of his mother Alice to whom he was very close. Fred went to the doctors and the usual response from the medical profession at that time was 'just get a grip of yourself man etc'.

Clearly Fred had what was known then as shell-shock and of course today it would have been known as post traumatic stress disorder. The term 'shell-shock' was coined in 1917 by a Medical Officer called Charles Myers. It was also known as 'war neurosis' and latterly as 'combat stress' the only treatment was a period of rest and a stay in a mental hospital.

The First World War devastated the lives of a generation of young men, but the trauma of war didn't end when the guns stopped firing. Thousands of soldiers returned from the battlefields and trenches of the First World War reeling from the sheer horror of the conflict.

By the end of the war, 20,000 men were still suffering from shell-shock. Thousands more had experienced its symptoms during their military service. It is estimated that 80,000 had suffered during the period of the war.

Across the country, doctors were mystified by a condition that they hadn't seen before. Soldiers were returning from the trenches blind, deaf, mute or paralysed.

Doctors couldn't find any physical damage to explain the symptoms, these included hysteria and anxiety, uncontrollable diarrhoea, paralysis, limping and muscle contractions, blindness and deafness, nightmares and insomnia, heart palpitations, depression, dizziness and disorientation and loss of appetite.

This for many was the end of their days. Not able to leave the hospital, medical science had not identified this illness, for many only physical/visible wounds were real. Mental illness was marginalised with many more ex-soldiers suffering with this hidden illness than the system could cope with.

The treatment for this in the early 1900s would have been either the shaming of individuals, emotional deprivation or even worse, a type of bloodletting of the skull, a lobotomy which was believed to release the pressure from inside the brain causing the patient to return to normal. This was eventually proved to be utter rubbish and the effects of this lasted a lifetime for the individuals concerned.

A type of electric shock treatment was inflicted upon the victims believed at the time, to jolt their brainwaves back to normal. These early treatments did nothing to improve the recovery and wellbeing and in most severe cases the returning soldiers found themselves incarcerated in a mental hospital.

The system could not cope with the influx of these patients, although in 1914 there were one hundred and two hospitals looking after the mental health patients. In those were patients which today would not be deemed mentally ill, such as people with dementia, downs syndrome, liver disease and tuberculosis.

By the end of 1918, twenty new mental hospitals had either been built or mansion houses converted to handle the volume of new patients.

One of these hospitals was in Chartham near Canterbury, it was spread over a vast estate with beds for two thousand patients, this shows the scale of the problem.

Deaths within these hospitals increased due to cramped conditions, this was particularly prevalent during the flu epidemic of 1918/1919. It is interesting that the stigma of mental hospitals was so obvious then, the term 'war hospital' was used for the ones requisitioned for use exclusively for the returning mental health patients.

The reserves of internal strength would have been incredible, Fred would have realised that he had a problem but through sheer determination would have worked through it to raise his family and although he had issues with sleeping and nightmares, he worked through his problems and did a good job. In 1933 Fred joined the special constables in Folkestone, serving alongside the regular constables some of whom he had been in the army with fifteen years before.

Fred must have felt some trepidation when his eldest son Aubrey joined the Territorials in 1937 as the next war was looming.

The fathers of Fred's age would have seen that a war was coming and the memories of twenty years before would have been paramount. Looking at his son's enthusiasm and keenness to serve his country he would have been so proud but equally very fearful, based on his memories of the first war.

He would have joined up feeling the national fervour and gradually through his years of service would gradually have seen this eroded away. All he could hope for was that he came through unscathed.

World War 2

In early 1939 Fred's worst fears were realised, Aubrey was mobilised and as the newspaper cutting showed, his group of fellow soldiers looked keen and ready to take on whatever the world was going to throw at them.

An additional problem was manifesting itself. The family sent away their youngest son Dennis to Wales as part of the evacuee program. This was a period in Dennis's life he always considered the worst ever.

It caused the family more emotional turmoil, but as Folkestone was only twenty six miles across the sea from France, they could do no more to keep him safe. In late May 1940 the Local Defence Volunteers was formed and it absorbed all the special constables, so Fred was once again in an army uniform.

The Volunteers did not receive pay and were initially armed with pick handles before weapons were issued later in the year. The volunteers who had served in the first war helped to train the younger guys and those in reserve occupations, such as Fred had been during the early years of WW1.

Evenings and weekends were spent guarding the port, and training with the regular soldiers who were stationed at Shorncliffe. Eventually this force would be officially known as the 'Home Guard'.

Fred's sleeping pattern at this time became worse and the nightmares returned. Aubrey was posted away with his unit which was a heavy anti-aircraft battery. They initially went off to Twydall near Gillingham defending the naval base at

Chatham where they trained and prepared.

Aubrey wrote home regularly, but due to the censorship couldn't tell his parents where he was. Just before the war started the defences of the UK were ramped up and Aubrey's unit was posted to defend the ports of Dover and Folkestone.

This was ironic because although they were less than a mile from the family home, again Aubrey couldn't tell his parents. Then one day he had a few hours off and walked home with some of his friends. Aubrey would not see the family home again after this visit. Once again, the family would suffer another cruel blow in life.

After the evacuation of the British Expeditionary Force at Dunkirk, the Germans consolidated their forces along the channel coast and began to fire long range guns across the channel.

This was really no more than a nuisance, psychological warfare as we know it today. The residents of the coastal ports would have to carry their tin helmets and gas masks everywhere as these shells were fired in random groups.

For instance, four or five would come over in quick succession and then nothing for two days. Air raids also started and huge areas were flattened down by the harbour including all of North Street where Fred's father lived. Fred senior took what they could salvage and moved into 67 Warren Road.

At the end of December 1940, the family once again experienced disaster, a high explosive shell came across the channel and once again found the coal hatch on the side of the house. It exploded in the basement causing significant damage and fire. The family managed to escape with minor injuries, but the house was destroyed. They would never own another house again.

The final chapter

A tiny cottage was found to rent in the hamlet of Bramling by one of Rose's relatives. It was not large enough to house Fred senior, so he moved in with his sister in the village of Market Deeping in Lincolnshire whilst the family went to Bramling.

Bill joined the RAF shortly after this followed by Gladys in 1942. Myrtle cottages no longer exists. it forms part of a garden. Back in 1940, it was four tiny cottages right on the road, which eventually would be demolished in the 1960s as they were uninhabitable.

Furniture was donated by family and Fred managed to get a job at Miles builders in Wingham. As before in Folkestone, he assisted the adjoining undertakers as a pall bearer. The family settled into a new life in the country. Rose was from a family of farm workers so this transition was quite easy. Not so for Fred.

He had lived in a town all his life and was used to the constant noise and bustle of movement. Although they lived on the A257 then, it was a very quiet road and at night the only sound was from the owls in the wood opposite. This did nothing for Fred's state of mind.

The extreme quiet allowed memories from that awful time long ago to surface and nightmares and insomnia were a daily occurrence. Along the road was 'The Volunteer' public house and it was frequented by locals, many of whom had served in the first war so Fred felt it was a safe place with like-minded people.

Fred transferred to a local Home Guard company and

supported the local regiment guarding local important buildings and key points.

The day Fred had dreaded finally came. Aubrey had written to say he was going abroad in the new year of 1941 and on the twentieth July a telegram arrived saying he was missing in action.

Fred knew what that meant and tried to reassure the rest on the family, but inside he knew what was coming next and sure enough ten days later another telegram arrived stating that Aubrey had been killed in action in Crete.

Fred took to his bed distraught and the doctor was called. My mother Gladys, said he was never the same again. Fred had gone through many trials and tribulations throughout his life but nothing could have prepared him for the loss of his firstborn son to war. Fred became reclusive and emotional and for years took a 'potion' prescribed by his doctor.

Depression as we know it today set in and life for Fred was just survival. Fred was unable to continue with the Home Guard as the synergy with the uniform brought back too many unpleasant memories.

He spent a while in hospital with the official diagnosis as 'delayed shell-shock'. But Fred was grieving for his son with what seemed to be the weight of his early life bearing down on him with no end in sight.

Fred was like thousands of others from his generation. The horrors of war had left him with scars both physical and mental and despite his tenacity and drive the final straw had come and he needed time to come to terms with it.

Later in the year, Dennis returned from Wales and for a short while. the family were together in Bramling albeit a bit of a squeeze.

Fred had applied for compensation under the government compensation scheme and eventually a postal order arrived in the post for the sum of one hundred pounds.

This was the agreed amount under the rushed legislation for a four-bedroom house. Not a lot to show for all that loss including the property and belongings. It helped to tide the family over for the tough times ahead.

Fred became obsessed over Aubrey's final resting place. He wrote numerous letters to the War Office Casualty department over the months following the notification. The responses were somewhat vague because Crete had to be evacuated in a hurry. Anyone who had survived in Aubrey's unit was now in captivity and unable to tell their stories.

The Red Cross didn't get access to Crete until 1944 and by then Aubrey's remains had been moved at least twice. It wasn't until 1946 Fred was finally advised that his son was interred in the new Commonwealth War Graves Commission graveyard in Suda Bay.

Because of the nature of his death and subsequent moves he was deemed as unidentifiable. His headstone is annotated 'Known unto God' His name was engraved on the War memorial in Athens.

Finally, Fred could rest, the ferocity of his letter writing was driven and compulsive. This would have been fuelled by a huge envelope of his own letters written between March and July 1941 returned stamped unceremoniously as 'Killed in Action'

The effects of the gas on Fred's lungs reduced his ability to function and together with panic attacks left him breathless. This must have been so frightening as they mainly occurred in the middle of the night when he awoke from his unrelenting nightmares.

He was eventually admitted to the Lenham Sanatorium where he received treatment for his chest condition and some therapy for his mental health conditions. At that time Lenham was the counties only hospital specialising in lung conditions. It was set up in 1914 mainly for patients suffering from tuberculosis, but saw many patients over the years who had the same traumas as Fred.

Fred eventually went back to work at Miles builders and by now, had become quite an accomplished carpenter and worked on many local building contracts which are still evident as you travel the local area. Fred was a dab hand at making roof trusses which today are massed produced and delivered wholesale.

Fred never recovered from Aubrey's loss and was relieved when Gladys and Bill returned from service in 1945. The hamlet of Bramling was part of the parish of Ickham and Well, and in 1949 a letter arrived in the post from the parish council, requesting that Fred and Rose be the guests of honour at Ickham church at the unveiling of the new war memorial, followed by a reception with local dignitaries in the village hall.

Fred was initially pleased to be invited but with trepidation and a sense of loss, he decided not to attend. At the last minute he was convinced that it would be a good social occasion and the family went along. Fred pulled away the curtain hiding the memorial flanked by his wife and three children and many veterans of both world wars.

Dennis joined the post war RAF and became an air traffic controller. After leaving he joined the civil aviation authority and eventually retired as the most senior air traffic controller at Croydon airport.

Ill health meant he retired early but this coincided with the diminishing health of his mother Rose and eventually he became her full time carer until her death in 1979.

Fred was not a well man through his later years, his lung capacity reduced further and the complications that followed brought on chest infections and bouts of recurring pneumonia.

This was made worse by the living conditions in Myrtle cottages. The houses were built directly onto the chalk bank and damp and mould permeated through all the cottages. These were pulled down in the late 1960s as I alluded to earlier.

The damp conditions and predisposition to chest infections affected his ability to work and eventually on a doctor's recommendation they were allocated a council house in Littlebourne where they lived until 1970.

There weren't any military pensions then for disabled veterans so they had to rely on their savings until their old age pensions were available. The question of war pensions was addressed on demobilisation where everyone had to sign away any right to pensions unless they had a severe physical disability.

When I was born in 1957, we were living across the road to both of my grandparents. The Bennetts and the Garretts lived next to each other until the Bennetts managed to move to a council house in Ickham. As I grew up, I always felt that Fred distanced himself from me and I never understood why.

At an early age the Bennett grandparents were always full of fun and so indeed was my grandmother Rose, but grandad Garrett was always seemingly aloof and distant, trapped in his own thoughts. My mother always said 'don't worry it's all about the war', but now I wonder which war she was referring to.

It seemed that he had many wars going on in his head all at once. I always thought that he didn't like me and as a small child I couldn't understand why. He would always get up and walk out when we entered the house and he couldn't look at me.

It was only just before my mother's death I found out the truth. At every stage of my development I looked exactly like his son Aubrey and looking now at the family photos it's hard to tell us apart. It's only the faded photographic paper that gives a clue. Now some fifty five years later I understand the truth about my grandad.

Fred Garrett faced many disasters both personally and within the family. He must have had an unbelievable strength of character. Many an individual today would buckle at the first hurdle.

To have the loss of his home, income and business which would have set up the family for life gone in an instant, the horrors of the first World War, and a promising football career in tatters. He had to deal with the mental torture during the inter war years, then the loss of his house in Folkestone and then robbed of his eldest son, I don't know how he survived these traumas and still raised and provided for a family. His generation was made of more sterling stuff!

Fred would have learnt to cope with his illness, although he probably didn't think he was ill at all. Treatment for his illness and depression could have made a real difference to his life had he been alive today.

Drugs to help the depression and counselling fostering the practise of talking about experiences and sharing knowledge with others would certainly have helped. The new treatment to park memories in a different part of the brain has come on so much in recent years. I now know my grandad, Fred Garrett. The next time I pass through Ickham, I will stop at the church, visit his grave and tell him just that!

Chapter 2

The Newing family

The Newing family consisted of fifteen children although some died very young. I am grouping them together as their early years were very similar until their late teens onwards.

The head of the house was Charles Newing and together with his wife Jane, nee Prett, lived in a tied cottage with only two bedrooms. Charles was a farm labourer and eventually all the boys would follow suit mostly working at the same farm, Jacques Court, Bladbean near the village of Elham, just outside Folkestone.

The Newing's were considered lucky as all four of the brothers who went to war came back home. True, some received some horrendous wounds but all carried the war in their heads until the end of their days. Their parents must have seen such a change in them, and their siblings must have thought them very odd.

Before I continue, I must stress that the Newing boys all had a fiery nature and were very opinionated, which became more apparent when they returned from France.

Apart from Edwin, the other brothers were called up. In the early stages of the war farm labourers were exempt from service until the losses started to outweigh those who were joining. Both Charlie and John were in their twenties which was considered to be old amongst their peer group back in the day.

Chapter 3

Edwin (Ted) Newing, 1896-1954

Ted Newing volunteered for service and joined the 7th
(Service) battalion the Buffs and like so many before him
was sent to France. Details of his service are a little vague with
only the hearsay from relatives, and villagers from Elham who
remembered him.

The records were destroyed in the fire at the National
Archive storage units in South London1940. Some research
was possible with the aid of some books and war diaries. I
have established he was entitled to wear a wound strip which
he is wearing in his main photograph indicating the photo was
taken after his recovery.

Ted was at the first day of the Somme offensive. It must be
hard for us to relate what the scene was back then, the tales of

trenches and mud where far from the scene that Ted observed. The full horrors of the shelling and trench stalemate were yet to come to this quiet corner of the Somme valley in rural Belgium.

The war had been fought for some two years before this offensive, but the Somme valley had escaped the intensity of fighting and artillery barrages that befell other areas along the line.

The German troops had reinforced the area and had dug a defensive trench system down the valley. The scene the 7th battalion faced was one of grass meadows across rolling hills, not to dissimilar to Salisbury Plain.

On the first of July, summer flowers were in the fields and birds were singing all around. In particular, Skylarks would rise vertically from their nests singing until they were almost out of sight.

When the barrage started it threw up mounds of dirt and grass clumps. The troops advanced across the grassy fields, but as they neared the enemy the ground was becoming more pockmarked. Ted was wounded slightly before he reached the enemy defence line.

He was sent to the Field hospital and after recuperation returned to A Company 1st Buffs. He was sent to 1 platoon. 1st Buffs was in the thick of the action during September and October 1918 and it was during one of these actions that Ted was again wounded and suffered paralysis. Ted was lying in a shell hole for three days and unable to move or to speak.

He couldn't call for assistance. His company was cut off for a few days behind the German lines, so although he couldn't move, he was ignored by the opposing forces as they thought he was dead. It was on the third day the area was once again in friendly hands that a stretcher party out looking for wounded, spotted Ted opening and closing his hand as a signal to them.

The road back to recovery was a slow and painful one, with Ted being weak from loss of blood, serious facial injuries and a bullet wound to his upper arm and shoulder.

He passed back through the hospital system until he was moved to the paralysis hospital in North London. It was there that the first contact with his family was made after the initial War Office telegram stating he was missing in action.

Over the next year he moved around various hospitals in the UK and gradually his condition improved. At one convalescent hospital in Norfolk, Ted was cared for by a young nurse, Daisy Scrivener.

After his discharge in 1919 he moved back to the village of Elham. Daisy moved down shortly afterwards and was employed at the Radnor Park Hospital in Folkestone. Ted and Daisy married in 1924 and they moved to Southdown cottages in the Back Row in Elham.

Ted was unable to use his left arm which prohibited him returning to the land as a farm worker, but saw an opportunity to start his own business. The local sweet shop and tobacconist was available for lease as the owner was about to retire. Ted jumped at the opportunity with the existing incumbent able to teach him the business before he finally retired. Ted became very adept at holding a sweet jar under his limp arm whilst using his good hand to weigh out the contents.

Ted became like so many others of his generation, prone to nightmares and bouts of obsessive behaviour. For instance, his wife would always prepare his supper for about twenty minutes after he closed the shop and factored in the time it would take to walk the few hundred yards up to Southdown cottages where they lived.

After a few months he came home later and later, and Daisy would wonder why. Ted would lock the shop and walk up the hill, but in that down time his thoughts would always go back to the days of the war when he faced some of his darkest days.

In that short time, he would almost arrive at the steps of the house but couldn't remember whether he had locked the shop, so he would go back and check. This could happen three or four times before he would finally get home.

The sweet jars would always be lined up exactly and everything would be in its place. Ted had developed an almost obsessive compulsion. Today this would have been known as OCD (obsessive compulsive disorder), but back then he was thought just be a little odd.

Ted was well liked around the village. he grew up locally so knew most of the residents of his generation. For many years he kept the little shop going but his health deteriorated and he had to give up the lease of the business.

The mental health problems that tormented him became worse and he sought solace in alcohol which heightened all the problems. Fortunately, Daisy was a nurse who understood what Ted was going through having seen it first-hand many years before with returning servicemen in the hospitals where she worked. It must have been very tiring.

Ted eventually passed away in 1954 at the age of fifty seven. He had carried his demons for many years which ultimately contributed to his early death. Ted like so many others, suffered the effects of war for the rest of his life. He was one of the lucky ones, so many more men came back and fought the war every night until the day they died.

Suicide rates in younger men rose sharply after World War 1 but the medical care was not there for them. Although lessons were learnt and the care and treatment had come on in leaps and bounds since the Crimea and Boar wars, it was still very primitive. It was not until after World War 2 that the treatment became more joined up.

The National Health service was formed in 1948 and Mental Health services started to provide more consistent and appropriate treatment. The long term damage by then was done and Ted refused the treatment which would have resulted in him being an in-patient in a hospital. Ted by this time was just too world weary.

Chapter 4

Edward John (John) Newing, 1893-1951

Called up 19/1/17

John was called up for service to the Royal Garrison Artillery in 1917 at the age of twenty four, but on enlistment it was deemed that he was more suited to the Labour Corps, in particular an Agricultural company due to his experience as a farm hand and horseman. These companies were formed of older men either conscripted or from recovering wounded or those likely to be ill for a period of time.

They worked the land to ensure that the food was produced and the heavy farm work was completed. Although many women worked the land there were some jobs that need a man's expertise and strength. These companies worked mainly in the UK but quite a few were posted to France to assist the local farmers to produce food for our troops. It was to one of these companies 426, that John was posted and cap badged The Queen's Own Royal West Kent regiment.

Although the main role was to tend the land there were occasions when they were used in conjunction with the labour corps. This was to improve trench systems and defences prior to attacks and to repair rear areas following heavy shelling.

When digging and extending trenches in areas where fighting and shelling had occurred, these digging parties would uncover partly decomposed bodies covered by the fallout of shell explosions or covered by the deep mud of the trench systems.

The working parties would be heard by the Germans who would shell the rough area where the digging was heard causing casualties. This shelling took its toll on the younger men, particularly the ones who had not lived in the trench systems. If you were manning trenches you eventually became used to the sounds and took cover accordingly.

No matter how many times a spade would uncover a grisly reminder of previous battles, the shock and surprise would have affected even the most battle hardened veteran. At this point it should be remembered that for three years the war had ebbed and flowed over the same piece of ground with particularly wet winters.

Many things became buried in the mud which had dried out hiding its secrets until either being accidently discovered or indeed 100 years later when the area was being dug for footings to provide housing.

It seems that John was sent to a field hospital where he spent some time. The records don't show a physical injury or wounds, so he probably suffered an episode of 'shell-shock' or 'trench fever' as it was known then. There is no doubt his war service contributed to his behaviour and demeanour throughout the rest of his life.

His sister Phoebe used to say he was awake in the night with severe insomnia and used to walk around the house, pacing and talking to himself. It must have been very a worrying time for her. Of the Newing brothers, John was deemed the most sensible and level headed. The other brothers were opinionated and loud, John withdrew into himself and was quiet and became somewhat of a loner.

When he moved to Snow Cottage in Ickham he worked part time for Trevor Champion at Treasury farm doing general labouring and repairing machinery. John had grown up with heavy horses providing the transport and power. He was out of his depth with the tractors and machinery that were taking over the heavy work following the Second World war.

John eventually retired and spent his day walking around the village, sitting on the bench on the village green deep in his thoughts and memories.

He was known to have the *'thousand yard stare'*, the stare was common with shell-shock victims. It manifested as someone looking into the middle distance as if in a trance, with them not being able to bring themselves round to a normal state.

One therapy for this is to bring a sufferer back to reality this is known as 'grounding'. A technique to achieve this these days is to look around and say out loud five objects out loud they can see, asking them to say four things they can hear such as a clock ticking or a car engine.

Also ask them to touch three things, smell two distinct smells such as herbs in the garden or deodorant and finally describe a taste such as tea or toothpaste. This will help to ground a sufferer.

Night time brought the memories of his war service back and it was unrelenting. He must have been permanently tired and exhausted. Having to put up with his brother Charles, who was so highly strung, must have been very wearing for him.

Chapter 5

Charles Newing, 1891-1958

Charles was known all through his life as Charlie, he was a highly-strung person who was always doing something and could never rest. He was the hyperactive member of the family. Charlie worked the land along with his siblings and was eventually called up in September 1916 into the Royal Garrison Artillery was soon posted to an Agricultural company in France.

As with his brother John, Charlie was deployed to raise crops to feed the soldiers in France in order to cut down the massive cost of transporting food across the English Channel. Not much is known about his service other than he too was exposed to the realities of war many times during his time in France.

I stated earlier that the records of thousands of servicemen from this period were lost in a fire at the National archives in

Kew caused by an incendiary bomb in the early 1940s. Many of the records left are now digitised but woefully incomplete. It seems only the medal cards remain untouched as they were stored in a different area.

After the war Charlie was demobilised and returned to Elham and the farm he knew so well. In 1945 his mother Jane passed away. This hit Charlie hard, he became more withdrawn, agitated and random in his behaviour. The medicine of the day had no effect. Charlie used to believe that people were watching him and intent on doing him harm. These days he would have been diagnosed with psychosis, which at the time went untreated.

The family moved to White Cottage in Bramling around 1935 and shortly after arrival Charlie started to self medicate with alcohol. The local public house, 'The Volunteer', was just a short distance from the family home. This had an adverse effect by increasing his depression and worsening his state of mind.

One evening, he bundled up anything of value in the house, taking jewellery, watches, silver vases and both his and his brother John's medals etc, and burying them in Hazeling woods at the rear of the house. 'They were coming to get them' and wanted to save the family valuables before they arrived.

He was not in the house in the morning and after an extensive search Charlie was found the other side of the Adisham downs in a total state of confusion.

Later that day he was admitted to the mental hospital at Chartham where rudimentary treatment was performed. The family searched the woods for months looking for the signs of digging but to no avail. Charlie had no recollection of doing this and could offer no solution to finding them. The wood was pulled up in the late 1960s and is now part of many acres of apple orchards belonging to the Twyman family.

Newing family often wondered if the valuables were ever found or will they lay covered until some archaeologist unearths them in the next few hundred years. Charlie was eventually released and moved in with his brother and sister in the village of Ickham where he lived his life in turmoil. The psychosis remained for the rest of his life together with severe depression. He was committed to St Augustine's hospital in 1940 where he remained until his death in 1958.

A phrase used by many people which is both cruel and inhuman is the term 'village idiot' coined by people who hadn't experienced the war. They didn't possess the skills to connect with the hundreds of thousand ex-servicemen who like Charlie, wandered the streets talking to themselves and who were unable to converse sensibly upon being asked a question.

Many sad souls in this position were disowned by their families who again didn't have the understanding to cope with this terrible and debilitating illness. Many committed suicide and others were sent to prison for minor crimes. Others ended up in long term mental institutions.

Charlie is buried in Ickham Churchyard sharing a grave with his brother John. It seems that people who are highly strung in youth are more susceptible to mental illness in later life. This is amplified by exposure to the sights and sounds of war.

If he had lived during a different time, Charlie would undoubtedly have been diagnosed with several forms of mental illness and his psychosis would have been treatable. His case was amplified by what is now known as PTSD from his time spent in France.

Chapter 6

Frederick G Newing, 1894-1960

Called up 10/9/16

Fred Newing worked at Jacques Court before the war as a heavy horseman. His skill in breaking young horses was legendary locally. I suppose he would have been known as a horse whisperer by todays' terms. Fred received his mobilisation papers and the Army seized upon his skill with horses. Several million horses were being used for the war effort and they needed to be trained to work in harness.

Fred was recruited into the Royal Artillery, but fast tracked through basic training so he was able to put his skills to work quickly. On completion of this training he was posted to Polo Farm near Canterbury. This was a main depot for new intakes of horses for the Royal artillery, all of these animals were destined for the army in France. Fred was very good at his job and became the most skilful horseman in the depot.

Fred was a typical Newing though, opinionated and head-strong. There was an incident in France which displays this but I will mention it in detail shortly.

After the horses had been trained to work in harnessed teams they were shipped out to France by a convoluted route. They were taken by road in teams of eight in their harnesses, with one man riding the lead horse. They rode to Wingham railway station, some five miles away and loaded up into special wagons and taken with their riders to Shepherdswell station. There the wagons were connected to larger trains on the main line and taken to Dover.

On arrival in France they were taken to a holding area to await the call for reinforcement gun teams. The timescales were quite long even by todays standard's as horses need feeding, watering and rest according to the strict rules set down by the Ministry of War. I guess this was to ensure the horses were kept in tip top condition etc.

From leaving the depot at Polo Farm, it was about ten days before they would be delivered to the artillery units.

The incident I alluded to earlier was always the subject of discussion throughout the family for years. Fred had to deliver a group of horses to the front which was unusual as they were normally needed at the rear areas.

During one offensive the Germans pushed forward creating a bulge in the front line, sometimes known as a salient. They sometimes were dangerously near the allied rear areas which were less defended.

Two-gun teams had recently been killed, on arrival in the

rear area, they were urgently needed in the forward area. Fred and his team together with another one, had to deliver the horses to the gun line to tow back two guns which were dangerously exposed and unable to move. Fred and his colleague went forward at some speed but German machine gun fire opened up and killed the eight horses and their rider instantly just a few yards ahead of Fred.

The machine gun team was around two hundred yards away in a hollow. As they had broken through recently, there were no trenches on this salient and everyone in the rear area was dangerously exposed. Fred watched this unfold in front of him and became utterly incensed.

He seemed to care more about his animals than his friends and to see eight of them killed was more than he could cope with. He turned the gun team towards the machine gun and galloped at full speed towards them and ran them over killing all three Germans.

Fred then returned and linked up both guns to his team in tandem and towed them to safety. There were no officers present only senior non-commissioned officers who tried to get him a medal but alas were not successful, due to the rules regarding officers having to witness acts of bravery on the front lines.

Fred continued to train horses until the end of the war and once they had all been returned and the depot closed, did he demobilise.

Fred returned to Elham full of anger and remorse that he couldn't save the lives of his colleague and the horses. He was quite handy with his fists and this was often the cause of trouble with him at closing time at the local pub.

In 1921, Fred married Frances (Dolly) Goldfinch and they

moved to a tied cottage near Goodnestone to work as the horseman for Lord Fitzwalter. This he did for many years in between the wars but the old demons came back to haunt him. His behaviour became erratic and one day he had a confrontation with the farm manager which didn't end well.

The Fitzwalter Arms pub was only about one hundred meters from his home and he probably spent far more time there than he should have. The effects of alcohol can allow hidden memories to surface and Fred suffered mentally, having sleep problems and random attacks of anger and rage.

Fred was given the job of gamekeeper to keep him away from the farm manager who he had punched in the pub a few days earlier. Fred was well thought of and Lord Fitzwalter was reluctant to sack him.

When Fred retired, he was allowed to stay in the cottage as by then, the need for farm hands was diminishing. Tractors were taking over the work of horses. The old age pension was not enough to survive on so Fred resorted to poaching pheasants and other game on the estate. This put food on the table and money in his pocket from selling game in the local pub, right under the nose of Lord Fitzwalter! Fred became known as 'Slip Newing' due to his uncanny ability not to get caught stealing birds. Everyone knew he was doing it but he was never caught!

Fred, as with his brothers changed following his return from the war. He became more aggressive and angrier in later life remonstrating with anyone who looked at him. These days he would be given anger management treatment and counselling for his illness. Following that day in France, albeit fifteen minutes of terror, the anger and near hysteria stayed with him for the rest of his life.

In many ways the Newing family suffered more than most families in the longer term. Names on the war memorial faded and parents passed away releasing the burden of memories, but the Newings' carried the burden for everyone in their heads. This was not unusual, many communities, villages and towns across the UK had waved young soldiers away to do their patriotic duty, seeing them return a few short years later carrying with them hidden demons. Of course, a great proportion of returning soldiers were absolutely fine and managed to place their memories in a safe place within their souls to lead a normal life.

This generation of warriors over the next few years brought up a new generation of youngsters who in a few short years would be the cream of the country's soldiers off to fight another world war. Sadly, which the horrors and disaster are still within memories of a few old men and women, who stand on Remembrance Sunday with their medals, straight and proud.

Chapter 7

Gladys Garrett, 1923-2009

'My Mother'

Gladys was the only girl in the family and nearly didn't make it to adulthood. Her three siblings took her to the Warren in Folkestone but she slipped on the rocks and fell into the sea. Gladys couldn't swim and it was only Bill's quick thinking that saved her from drowning. Gladys had a fear of water all her life following this incident.

Gladys left school at fifteen and worked as housekeeper and chef for the local vicar at St Mary's church in Folkestone, even though it was only just down the road Gladys lived in at the vicarage.

When Aubrey was killed Gladys wanted to join up and support the war effort. Both parents were against this but

Gladys was now eighteen so able to sign on without parental consent. Gladys went by train to the main recruiting office in Chatham on the twenty third of February 1942, thirty two years later to the day, I signed on at the same office for my short career in the RAF!

After the basic training at Morecambe, Gladys trained as a balloon operator, very soon being promoted to look after a section of operators. On promotion she was deployed to the River Clyde protecting the convoys of American soldiers that were starting to arrive in preparation for the invasion of Europe.

In March 1944 the need for balloon protection was diminishing as the enemy air threat was becoming less of a problem. The WAAF balloon crews were disbanded and re mustered. Gladys chose to be a radio operator and went to RAF Cosford and just scraped a 43% pass on Morse code.

Gladys was then posted to North Coates in Lincolnshire working in the Operations room sending messages to and from the Bomber crews on their missions every night. Eventually her final posting was RAF Langham in Norfolk.

On the twenty sixth of March 1945 life would never be the same again for Gladys Garrett. The night shift crews changed at midnight and after a cup of tea with her two colleagues, she cycled the three miles back to her billet on an adjacent RAF station.

In those days the RAF personnel and the WAAF's were kept separate so they could stay at the base where they worked. It must have been tiring to work twelve hour shifts and have to cycle three miles back to their billets.

At 01.48am, a Wellington bomber was seen to be in trouble on take off. One of the two engines lost power and the aircraft failed to gain height. The pilot struggled to maintain control and gain enough height for the crew to bail out and it subsequently crashed in a field about half a mile away from the road where the girls were cycling home.

The three girls plus a WAAF ambulance driver who was on her way to the medical centre at Langham, rushed across the fields to see if they could help. The four girls managed to pull the crew from the wreckage despite a fire in the fuel tanks.

Bombs and ammunition were exploding while they were inside the aircraft. They managed to drag three of the crew out alive, but severely injured. They then went back inside to retrieve the four members of the crew who had died, they just managed to do this before the aircraft exploded.

The ambulance driver was WAAF Sergeant Ivy Cross. She performed a similar rescue just a week later in identical circumstances and was rightly awarded a British Empire medal for her courage.

Gladys was quite distraught following her part in the first rescue. The gold watch she was wearing which her brother had given her just before he embarked to Egypt and his fateful onward journey to Crete, was missing so this added to her problems.

The girls were filthy and their uniforms torn and burnt. They were debriefed and went to the medical centre to have the burns, cuts and scratches attended to and sent to bed just before dawn.

For some reason the WAAF hierarchy didn't inform the girls' work station and when they failed to arrive for work at 12pm the next day there was hell to pay. It took some time to explain the nights activities and eventually the girls were given two days off.

Gladys caused a bit of fuss and upset because of this was threatened with disciplinary action. Having handled the wounded and killed aircrew played on her mind, picking up an arm or a leg where the burnt flesh would peel away in her grip was something a young girl should not have to face.

Together with the loss of the watch which was irreplaceable, events played on her mind and she had a short term mental breakdown. The RAF in its wisdom thought she should just 'man up' as it's known today, and pull herself together.

The aftermath of serious incidents with service personnel are treated so differently now, a group get together and a chat with all the support services present mostly gives the closure that personnel need. Gladys was reduced in rank from corporal to AC2 (the lowest rank possible) and fined a significant amount of wages. This was a very cruel outcome following a very brave and frightening time in her life.

After discharge Gladys returned home and worked for a local farmer as housekeeper and cook in the village to where her parents had moved. After my parents married the first signs of problems raised their head. Gladys had a series of miscarriages, and she became very angry at the slightest thing. She had insomnia and started to drink quite heavily. The doctors decided it was just hormones after the miscarriages and dismissed it offhand.

Following my birth, the mental health issues seemed to reduce, but in my teens, they became more evident. Broken sleep patterns, unexplained outbursts, moodiness and random tearfulness. My mother and father ran the local shop in Ickham until 1991 when they retired. Gladys was always pleasant and kind to her customers but this was just a front, after all, her mother was a Newing!

In her later years she had Alzheimer's and dementia, this had the effect of lowering her guard. As a shopkeeper she had to have a pleasant demeaner and be nice and polite to all her customers, almost a false appearance as she hid her true feelings. Gladys became opinionated and sometimes quite rude whilst in the care of the support services. Her distant memories of her time in the WAAF became clear memories and she relived her experiences on a daily basis.

We found out that Gladys had a boyfriend to whom she was very close, he was in 4 Buffs the local TA infantry unit. He was sadly killed in France just before the evacuation of the British Expeditionary force. This affected Gladys very badly and the memories of this returned in later life once the dementia had taken over. In her later days in a care home she rarely slept and relived that period of time over and over again in her mind.

If Gladys had received a period of wind down after the incident there may have been a chance that she would have come out of this with only a few distant memories, but the pain and hurt of being disciplined and reduced in rank was one straw too far.

Chapter 8

John F. Bennett, 1957-

I was fortunate to be able to live the dream every Territorial Army soldier aspires to and be selected to go to Kosovo in 2001 with our sister battalion, 1 PWRR. I was asked to deploy on a voluntary basis rather than be mobilised, to write a paper on the deployment process which at that stage was a little disjointed.

Mobilisation through the centre at Chilwell was sometimes hit and miss so the hierarchy needed an independent report on how it could be more efficient.

I did some pre deployment training with the RAF for three days and shortly afterwards I flew to Pristina to join the rest of the battalion who had been in theatre for a couple of weeks before I arrived.

This was my first operation after twenty-one years in the Territorial army, although I was an experienced officer, I was a little nervous at what I would face. Because I had to write a paper about the mobilisation the battalion felt I should be exposed to as much variation as possible.

My job was to command the operations room from 4pm through to 11pm. Anything outside these hours I could latch on to whatever I felt would be beneficial for my experience.

It didn't start too well. After I had unpacked and was just dozing off, and there was a huge bang in the courtyard below me. A patrol had just returned and the guys were unloading their rifles in the specially constructed bay below my window.

One of the French commandos attached to the battalion didn't follow the correct drills on his rifle and a bullet came through the window, a few inches above my head and buried itself in the ceiling!

I did my job and became involved in patrols, searches and meeting the population. A full scale exercise took place in the only power station in the country regarding storage of chemicals. That was interesting and informative.

One day I went on a patrol in the café district in Pristina, and as we rounded the corner to the main square the sound of gunfire stopped us in our tracks. A guy was holding an AK47 assault rifle and on the floor in front of him was another guy lying dead.

We called out to the belligerent and asked him to put down the weapon but he seemed frozen to the spot unable to move, probably through shock. The patrol covered me and I walked slowly up to him and took the rifle from him. The guys with me plasticuffed him and we awaited the police to arrive.

I had the shakes back at the operations room whilst being debriefed which was uncontrollable, although I felt fine and in control, the tremors lasted most of the day.

I worked as ADC to Ronnie Flanagan for a few days during a military/police operation, prior to this period he had recently retired as Chief Constable of the RUC. This brought a different perspective to the way the military worked with the civil authorities and became so very useful during my military service later during my career.

Another incident that comes to mind was where I had to shoot a huge dog that was heading towards me teeth ready to tear me to pieces. It was a bull mastiff type dog and we had been told to avoid dogs as most had rabies and worse! I was running away and couldn't cock my pistol quickly and only just managed to deal with the dog, just as it was close enough to hear its breathing!

Several more incidents occurred during my time in Kosovo but when my time came to return home I was transported to the airport and returned to Brize Norton in Oxfordshire.

The next day I was back to work, inspecting customers' damaged cars. After a couple of hours, I just sat in my car feeling shocked and helpless, two days before I was dealing with shootings and rocket propelled grenade incidents, together with protection of politicians and dignitaries and here I was, dressed in my suit discussing a car park dent with a rude customer.

I couldn't get out of operations mode. I was jumping at bangs and loud voices, vehicles approaching at speed sent me into apoplexy.

I spoke to my manager about it and he didn't understand what I was trying to tell him. I finally understood how my relatives must have felt when returning from wars in far distant lands, and the frustration they must have felt unable to explain how they were feeling.

I went to see my doctor and explained how I felt, he prescribed anti depressant medication which I was sure would not help so I didn't take them. I wrote the paper for the mobilisation centre, and stressed the need for a wind down period after an operation so military personnel can mentally prepare themselves for the perceived mundane world they return to.

It took me a couple of years to get it out of my system and this took its toll on my family.

Now it's clear some fifteen years later that I suffered with an adjustment disorder which was pretty much unheard of back in 2002. The physical and emotional symptoms fitted my profile to a tee.

Service personnel have a unique view on life with almost a fatalistic approach. Some have seen terrible things and after that you become almost invincible until something goes wrong, and everything comes tumbling down.

Chapter 9

Conclusions drawn

There was a stigma attached to mental health until recently, people with issues were rarely spoken of within families, it is also interesting that the story of John and Charlie was never mentioned after they had had passed away, almost as though they had never existed. Pure embarrassment and shame I suppose by their remaining family members.

There are many myths about PTSD, but this is a generic assumption as not all cases fall into this category. Many returning soldiers returning from conflicts not only in WW1 but every conflict up until Afghanistan, had behavioural issues. This has recently been correctly named as 'Adjustment Disorder' which is what I suffered with.

After discharge you leave a close cossetted unit with food, medicine and pay provided as part of the service contracts, after discharge you had to start again.

For the two world wars, Korea and first Gulf war, the separation period from home was far in excess of the normal six months deployment we have now. In some cases, it was nearly six years away from home. Having been in service one day and back home the next was a tremendous shock to many.

Adjusting to family life, toning down language, getting a job and returning to the head of the household proved too much for some. Wives at home had been responsible for maintaining the household, raising the family usually on their own.

Suddenly their role was taken away by, in most cases, someone who was simply not yet ready to take back that role.

The media today has improved the awareness of mental illness in the veteran community. There are adverts at the train stations, along the underground escalators. Whole page adverts in the national newspapers and also is all over the facebook community.

Back in 1918 there was nothing. Soldiers were returning home probably unaware they had a mental illness. The common term for that generic mental illness was 'oh he has shell-shock!' almost inferring that the corner of the carpet had been lifted and the problem hidden away out of site.

Returning service personnel have so much access to help and assistance now. The transition from military life to civilian is a different experience to even five years ago. The NHS GPs are sent the medical documents of the soldiers on discharge or you simply advise them that you are ex-military and your notes are annotated as such.

A form is available from the gov.uk website to complete to obtain your records, and a consent form for the surgery. This means you get jumped to the head of the queue for specialist appointments and treatment for service related injuries or illness.

One example of this is physiotherapy. Normally the wait is around six weeks, but to ex-service men and women it can be less than a week based on the clinical need. There are ex-military doctors and surgeons within the NHS.

Some have received funding to set up clinics to sort out the all too frequent problems of worn out joints and provide new knees, hips where a lifetime of carrying and running with immense weights on their backs has taken its toll. This can be life changing.

Getting operations quickly can get veterans back in employment quicker and this in turn can improve the mental state of mind. One of these is the Chavasse clinic based in the Royal Sussex Hospital in Brighton.

The funding for mental health treatment and awareness for veterans has improved in the last two years. Regional teams who understand veterans and their problems have joined forces in the Armed Forces Network.

A series of champions are across the country in all areas of the NHS, Department of work and Pensions and Local Government departments for housing and benefits. They work to ensure the interests of veterans are taken into account and the unique problems they face are addressed.

The treatment for PTSD has advanced in leaps and bounds in the last ten years. This has brought help to thousands of ex and current serving members of the armed forces. This does not exclude the Fire, Police and Ambulance service personnel who also experience things that civilians should never see.

The number of veterans suffering flashbacks, depression, insomnia and mood swings following the end of World War 1 isn't documented as the illness wasn't recognised. The term 'Shell-shock' which today would be referred to as combat stress was a label given to those who couldn't function at all following discharge from the hospitals. Sadly, a high proportion of these men ended up in mental hospitals or sanatoriums. The amount of suicides in this group was very high.

Those veterans who were able to survive were treated as 'village idiots' subject to ridicule by those who didn't understand what horrors they had experienced throughout their wartime service.

Those who left the service showing no physical or mental scars would have returned to their previous lives with very few problems other than the reintegration into their old jobs and lifestyle, their lives would be different as the women at home were now more independent. They had run the home front for a number of years in the absence of their husbands.

As with today, the PTSD symptoms could be immediate or would manifest somewhere after twelve to fourteen years following service. Usually this would be triggered by a major life event such as a death of a close relative, divorce or loss of home and employment.

The latter was quite common after the two World Wars in rural areas as farm labourers were in tied cottages. The increase of farm machinery, and improved technology was starting to make the numbers of labourers needed to run a farm reduce exponentially after the Second World War.

There is a school of thought that if individuals have a pre-existing undiagnosed mental health condition, it becomes significantly reduced during service due to the regimented system which doesn't allow 'thinking time' to any degree. It is not until discharge that the original condition re-emerges with interest.

Sufferers could have a high dependence on alcohol and this would increase the effects of the illness. In order to survive, veterans would likely turn to petty crime and a journey through the courts and imprisonment would be the likely route.

There would have been a higher rate of suicides amongst this group of individuals. Statistics on veterans' suicides are not available for the veterans of World War 1 which are unfortunately only now being discussed.

We make assumptions that this group of veterans would be a high proportion of all suicides in the community during this era.

Oddly, there are many cases where soldiers return and have no effects whatsoever. But American D Day veterans calling the US veterans agency increased, after watching the opening ten minutes of the film Saving Private Ryan. This film was so realistic it brought out long forgotten memories leading to veterans calling the various help lines asking for help and assistance from the mental health services.

Annex A

As the story of Aubrey Garrett formed so much of the stories of my childhood and the generation before, I thought I would tell the history of this charismatic lad who never sought fame or the recognition for doing his duty. He was just another statistic of war.

Aubrey Charles Winter Garrett (1920-1941)

Aubrey Garrett joined the Territorial army in 1938 at the local drill hall in Folkestone. He worked as a general hand at the gas works in Foord Road in Folkestone since leaving school. He was a 'bit of a lad', a joker who was widely liked both by his civilian work colleagues and his TA counterparts.

I am sure Aubrey was very much aware of his father's activities during the First World War and being the oldest son, felt he had to 'do the right thing'. Any wise words from his father would have been dismissed with the exuberance of youth.

War was slowly approaching and even in 1937 the clouds were becoming darker on the short distance across the channel from Folkestone.

Aubrey was officially called up in 1939 and he reported to the drill hall with a spring in his step and a sense of excitement, not realising the concerns for his safety by his father who would have witnessed first-hand the same patriotism and the keenness of the younger generation at the start of World War 1. The eyes of the young men showed excitement and innocence, without realising at that moment the true horrors of what the next six years would bring upon the world. Things were never going to be the same again.

Aubrey, following various unit and individual training courses was deployed with his unit to the cliffs behind Dover to be part of the national defences. It must have been frustrating for the soldiers who lived in Folkestone not to be able to go home to see their families. Some were only a mile away from their comfortable beds, but such is call up. Once you have reported you could be sent anywhere.

One of the most ludicrous things which was spoken about was the visit by the King to the gun battery one day. The guns were laid in and the troops were at their stations. Every man doing his job but one tiny thing was wrong. The loaders were holding the shells ready to insert them into the breech, but thankfully they didn't need to fire in anger.

The new 3.7-inch calibre guns they had recently had delivered didn't have the ammunition to go with them. There were still the old three inch shells around the gun positions which of course were worse than useless! The King was very impressed by the unit efficiency but never knew that the guns could never be fired!

Fast forward to late 1940, the Battle of Britain was over and troops were being deployed to the middle east to address the threat from Hitler's troops in North Africa. 89 Regiment HAA (Heavy anti-aircraft) including 234 battery arrived in Suez in mid February 1941. After a few days of administration and acclimatisation, the batteries were deployed to protect airfields in North Africa.

The morning of the nineteenth of May 1941 brought a light wind from the west with clear skies. The troops who were not on guard did their ablutions and thought about breakfast. The deployment from Egypt had been made hurriedly, and someone didn't include field bakeries or a structured plan for rationing several thousand troops, so it was bully beef and biscuits again.

Three weeks earlier 234 Battery (Heavy anti-aircraft) deployed with full scales of ammunition to Crete following the fall of the Greek mainland. The island was thought to be significant as it was only two hundred miles from Egypt and could act as a supply base for Rommel's force in Libya when he moved east towards the oil fields.

The Battery was part of 89 Regiment which was a Territorial Army unit formed in the South East. They had acquitted themselves well during the Battle of Britain and then deployed to Africa to support the 8th Army. 236 and 238 Batteries remained to support the army in Africa and 234 was warned off to support the defence force in Crete.

The unit together with a hastily formed division (CREFORCE) under General Bernard Freyberg set up defensive positions around the capital Chania, the strategic deep water port in Suda Bay and the airfield at Maleme to the west. The areas of Heraklion and Rethmynion to the east were defended against a seaborne invasion.

Three troop positions of 234 Battery were set up and trenches dug on the northern ridge of Suda Bay. The guns were laid in. The hills were composed of volcanic rock and the digging was difficult. The trenches were not as deep as usual and irregular in shape.

The forthcoming invasion date was available to the allied force, General Freyberg was included in the ULTRA information decoded in Bletchley Park and following several logistic setbacks the date was fixed for the twentieth of May.

The soldiers would have known that battle would have been imminent and during the nineteenth, orders would have been disseminated and the troops briefed.

The RA anti-aircraft units' issue of personal weapons was minimal, one rifle per eight soldiers and one Lewis gun per battery.

During the night the Battery engaged some bombers on the final leg of their bombing run to Maleme airfield without success. This was the only action they saw in the battle for Crete.

At dawn on the twentieth, hundreds of JU52 aircraft full of German paratroops made their way to the drop zones, as they turned west over the northern peninsular and dropped to around one thousand feet, the gunners were ready for this, but when the aircraft came into range they were too low to engage effectively as their barrels could not be depressed that low. All they could do was watch the battle develop to the east.

Many Germans were killed during their descent on the drop zones as by coincidence they were landing directly on the most defended positions.

When the paratroops reorganised, they moved to take the objectives to allow the main force to land safely. This was the final time parachutists were used in their traditional role. General Karl Student and his men would be absorbed into the line infantry because of the high number of casualties. On the flat ground which is now Chania airport, glider troops landed and merged with the paratrooper remnants that had landed two hours earlier.

Gunner Aubrey Garrett was a loader in the gun troop over-looking the bay. When it became clear they could not make any difference they took to the trenches and awaited orders. The Germans advanced and because of the ground and the shape of the peninsular, there was no withdrawal route for the allies in the area.

The paratroops arrived in waves but the 3.7-inch guns could not depress their barrels low enough to engage the enemy. The hills around Suda Bay are very high and the guns were designed for firing upwards. The smaller calibre 40mm Bofors guns from the light Anti-Aircraft unit were protecting the airfield perimeter at Maleme some three miles away and were able to acquit themselves well.

After the initial parachute drop a divisional sized assault from glider borne troops landed on the flat ground which is now Chania airport, just half a mile from the gun positions. Realising they could not attack the enemy they took up defensive positions in the trenches and waited for the Germans to arrive. The positions were mortared heavily, everyone crouched down but casualties were sustained.

After a couple of hours, the mortars stopped and Aubrey was the first to his feet and looked over the top of the trench. At that moment one final mortar bomb fell and that was the end of him instantly. The German infantry then assaulted and silenced the few remaining rifles. They over ran the position and machine gunned the unarmed troops huddling in the trenches.

The Germans captured the battery shortly after and around fifty guys were killed and over thirty were wounded. The majority went into captivity and the wounded taken to the German first aid posts. Hasty burial parties were formed and all the dead were buried in makeshift graves on the hillside around the battery positions.

Field burials were completed and the soldiers went into captivity. Aubrey was then moved by the Germans in the next couple of years and because of the nature of his death, could not be formally identified.

When the Commonwealth War graves consolidated all the war dead after the end of the war, he was moved again into the Suda Bay cemetery into one of the seven hundred graves containing remains deemed as unknown or unidentified.

On Saturday eighteenth October 2014 John and Sue Bennett visited the Commonwealth War Graves Commission cemetery in Suda Bay and placed a poppy cross on one of the unmarked graves together with a photograph.

Following this they visited the only accessible gun position and repeated the ceremony. The other two sites now lie within the NATO base which runs along the coast at Suda Bay and inaccessible to civilian visitors.

I have written about Aubrey in some detail explaining his

life and eventual death because he formed such a silent part of my childhood and upbringing. Aubrey through his death was an integral part of the family's thoughts and decisions right up until the death of his last remaining sibling in 2009.

Although Aubrey's death was a well-known story in the family no details were really known. Back in 1999 I was living in Northbourne near Deal in Kent. Working from home, I would often see a sprightly elderly gentleman taking daily exercise along the road opposite where I lived. Some months later I happened to be in the front garden and the elderly gentleman walked by, he stopped and had a chat.

His name was Albert Glind. He had lived in the village all his life and worked on the local farms. In 1938 he joined the TA at the Sandwich drill hall. the unit was 234 battery 89 regiment HAA! He knew my uncle and remembered him well. This amazing meeting threw up information that eluded my family since 1941. Albert served with Aubrey in the gun positions above Suda bay and worked with the team firing at bombers flying over at about 19,000 feet.

Albert was a free spirit and escaped from captivity several times until eventually he was incarcerated in Colditz castle where he stayed until the castle was liberated in 1945.

This chance meeting with Albert unlocked many hours of stories about Aubrey and his colleagues which would never have happened. Albert had never received his medals and with his permission I wrote away for his medals and had them mounted for him. The year before he passed away, he wore them at the local church for remembrance Sunday I stood in my service dress next to him!

When the survivors who had escaped returned to Egypt, 234

Battery was removed from the order of battle forever.

Glossary of terms and statistics, comparisons and references

0 -9. 234 battery HAA (Heavy Anti-Aircraft), this unit was formed from the 2nd Kent Battery, 3rd Home Counties brigade Royal Field Artillery in 1939 when the need for anti-aircraft guns to defend the local ports was identified.

A. AC2 Aircraftsman/woman second class, the lowest rank in the Royal Airforce/Women's Auxiliary Air force. Generally, the rank upon entry and basic training before trade training is undertaken.

ADC. Aide-de-Camp is a term for a personal assistant for someone of high military rank or a member of the Royal Family.

B. The Buffs, nickname for the Royal East Kent Regiment, the 3rd of foot. Taken from the uniform jacket facings around the time of the Peninsular war, which were buff coloured as opposed to the traditional red. 10 Battalions were raised for WW1

C. Chavasse Orthopaedic Clinic. The clinic is located within the Royal Sussex Hospital in Brighton. It was named after Captain Noel G Chavasse VC and Bar. Captain Chavasse was an eminent orthopaedic surgeon prior to the First World war who lost his life in 1917. At the time of print the clinic is run by Lieutenant

Colonel Ben Caesar, an Army Reserve Orthopaedic surgeon working within the NHS. https://www.bsuh.nhs.uk/chavasse-clinic/

D.   Lieutenant Donald Dean won his Victoria Cross for his actions over the 24-26 September 1918. Donald Dean was a Territorial Army officer from a Kentish family who owned a brick works in Sittingbourne. He went on to command a battalion in the Pioneer Corps during WW2 and eventually retired as the Lord Lieutenant of Kent. The following link describes the battle and his medal citation. http://www.victoriacross.org.uk/bbdeand.htm

H.   Home Guard (initially Local Volunteers or LDV) was an armed citizen militia supporting the British Army during the Second World War. Operational from 1940 to 1944, the Home Guard had 1.5 million local volunteers otherwise ineligible for military service, such as those who were too young or too old to join the regular armed services (regular military service was restricted to those aged eighteen to forty one) or those in reserved occupations. Excluding those already in the armed services, the civilian police or civil defence, approximately one in five men were volunteers. Their role was to act as a secondary defence force in case of invasion by the forces of Nazi Germany and other Axis powers. Lobotomy, is a form of psychosurgery, a neurosurgical treatment of a mental disorder that involves severing connections in the brain's prefrontal cortex. Most of the connections to and from the prefrontal cortex, the anterior part of the frontal lobes of the brain, are severed. The term is derived from the Greek word Lobos which means to cut or sever.

L.   The Labour Corps cooked, cleaned, carried and cared for the soldiers on the front line and behind the lines. They built roads and railways, carried the wounded and buried the dead. Men and women from across the Commonwealth made a vital contribution to the war effort as workers. Soldiers recovering from wounds or illness were sometimes attached to the Labour Corps companies, to assist the war effort before returning to their original units.

M.   Morse code is a method used in telecommunication to encode text characters as standardised sequences of two different signal durations, called dots and dashes or dits and dahs. Morse code is named for Samuel F. B. Morse, an inventor of the telegraph.

O.   Orbats. Military shorthand for Order of Battle, units attached or detached from a formation, battlegroup or unit.

P.   Pristina, capital city of Kosovo, population of 180k in 2002.

Plasticuff, a giant cable tie sometimes known as a zip clip. Generally used to tidy electrical cables.

Psychosis is a mental health problem that causes people to perceive or interpret things differently from those around them. This might involve hallucinations or delusions.

The two main symptoms of psychosis are:

Hallucinations – where a person hears, sees and, in some cases, feels, smells or tastes things that do not exist outside their mind but can feel very real to the person affected by them. a common hallucination is hearing voices.

Delusions – where a person has strong beliefs that are not shared by others. a common delusion is someone believing there's a conspiracy to harm them.

The combination of hallucinations and delusional thinking can cause severe distress and a change in behaviour.

Experiencing the symptoms of psychosis is often referred to as having a psychotic episode.

PTSD, Post-traumatic stress disorder (PTSD) is an anxiety disorder caused by very stressful, frightening or distressing events.

Symptoms of post-traumatic stress disorder (PTSD)

Someone with PTSD often relives the traumatic event through nightmares and flashbacks, and may experience feelings of isolation, irritability and guilt.

They may also have problems sleeping, such as insomnia, and find concentrating difficult.

These symptoms are often severe and persistent enough to have a significant impact on the person's day-to-day life.

R.   The Royal Garrison Artillery (RGA) was formed in 1899 as a distinct arm of the British Army's Royal Regiment of Artillery serving alongside the other two arms of the Regiment, the Royal Field Artillery (RFA) and the Royal Horse Artillery (RHA). The RGA were the 'technical' branch of the Royal Artillery who were responsible for much of the professionalisation of technical gunnery that was to occur during the First World War. It was originally established to man the guns of the British Empire's forts and fortresses, including coastal artillery batteries, the heavy gun batteries attached to each infantry division and the guns of the siege artillery.

RUC. Royal Ulster Constabulary, this was known as the Police Service of Northern Ireland from 2001.

S. Salient, a bulge in the enemy front line where offensive action caused the enemy to take ground in otherwise friendly areas behind the front lines.

The term 'Shell-shock' was coined when individuals who had been exposed to loud and continuous explosions became overcome initially with fear which quickly changed into a state of bewilderment, loss of physical control, total uncontrollable numbness and inability to communicate at any level. Shell-shock is eloquently described in the BBC archives with references to notable establishments contained within this link. http://www.bbc.co.uk/insideout/extra/series-1/shell_shocked.shtml#startcontent

Shell-shock was deemed serious enough during the war to have a book written about it. It was termed then as a hysterical disorder. https://archive.org/details/

T.   Territorial Force (TF), Created in 1908 as a volunteer reserve for the regular army by The Haldane reforms merging the previous militia and various Yeomanry units. In 1921 it became the Territorial Army which eventually became the army reserve in the mid 2000's.

Theatre. Used in the context of theatre of operations, an area where military operation is undertaken.

The Queen's Own Royal West Kent Regiment was a line infantry regiment of the British Army based in the county of Kent in existence from 1881 to 1961. The regiment was created on 1 July 1881 as part of the Childers Reforms, originally as the Queen's Own (Royal West Kent Regiment), by the amalgamation of the 50th (Queen's Own) Regiment of Foot and the 97th (The Earl of Ulster's) Regiment of Foot.

W.   WAAF Women's Auxiliary Air Force

Y.   Ypres is a town in Belgium which many of the German offensives were centred. Mustard gas was used in this area by the German army for the first time in the war.

Z.   Zeppelin airship. The Zeppelins were designed by the German aristocrat Count Von Zeppelin who patented the design in 1895. They were a rigid style airship filled with sealed airbags full of hydrogen gas. The German military seized on the design for offensive bombing operations. After WW1 the design was developed by other countries but it became out of favour after the

R101 and Hindenberg disasters in the 1920's.

Zeppelin L14 dropped bombs on the Army camp at Otterpool together with random drops on the racecourse and the town. Reference http://www.iancastlezeppelin. co.uk/1314-oct-1915-1/4587687739

Further resources are available via these web links.

https://www.giveusashout.org/get-help/?gclid=EAIaIQobChMI-uOi2nL3O5wIVjbHtCh0BtQKnEAAYASAAEgKko_D_BwE

https://allcallsigns.org/

https://www.combatstress.org.uk/get-help

https://www.bigwhitewall.co.uk/contact-us/

Photographs

Photograph of Aubrey Garrett at the drill hall on call up courtesy of Gerry Warren, KM group of newspapers. The photograph of the press cutting of the balloon crew handover, courtesy of the Sunday Mail. Remaining documents and photographs are owned by the author from the Garrett/Newing family archive

Fred Garrett outside the antique shop at 37 High Street (now known as the Old High Street) In this photograph he was about seventeen years old.

37 The high street as it is today, still a thriving business

Fred Garrett (centre of middle row) with Folkestone
Town football club celebrating winning the St Peters
league 1910/1911

Platoon photograph, 3 platoon 11 RWK Fred Garrett far right sitting on the grass. Note the size of the platoon, forty nine men and one Officer

A professional photograph taken of Fred Garrett after he joined the 11th (Lewisham) battalion of the Royal West

Kent's. The stick he is holding is known as a swagger stick. Soldiers on leave or 'walking out' would have to carry one. It was to stop soldiers putting their hands in their pockets! It was carried under the right arm, horizontal to the ground gripped at the end. It encouraged the soldier to swing their arms.

Fred and Rose Garrett taken in 1919 shortly after they were married.

Edwin (Ted) Newing, photograph taken when on leave, probably just before joining 7th Buffs, note the wound stripe on his left arm, and the wear on his boots!

Ted Newing rear rank indicated with an x. It is believed this was taken at Warminster prior to the battalion's deployment to France.

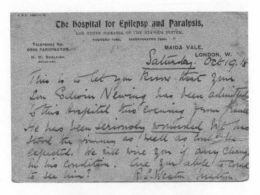

The card received by Jane Newing advising that Edwin was in hospital seriously wounded. It is not known if she visited him.

Fred and Dolly Newing. Taken on leave in 1918. Note the swagger stick. Fred's uniform differs from the infantry style, he is wearing jodhpurs more comfortable when riding horses.

Fred Newing in later years working on Lord Fitzwalter's estate at Goodnestone with his horses.

Edward John Newing (John) aged fourteen.

Charlie Newing, photo taken after the First World War.
The fear, confusion and terror are etched on his face
and in his eyes in this picture.

White Cottage Bramling. This is where the Newing
family moved to in the mid 1930s and where
my parents lived after they married in 1952.

This is a drawing/watercolour of Myrtle Cottages in Bramling painted by my father, Fred Bennett. It was directly opposite White Cottage. There were four cottages in this tiny block at any one time there would be four families of at least six living in two bedrooms.

Photograph published in the Folkestone Herald of the mobilisation of 234 battery RA in 1938. Aubrey Garrett 4th from right in the front rank.

AC2 Gladys Garrett, taken at Morecambe
during basic training.

FORGOTTEN HEROES

Hand-over. An RAF balloon crew salute a WAAF team who have come to relieve them

Press cutting courtesy of the Daily Mail. The WAAF
crew handing over to the incoming RAF crew.
The corporal saluting is Gladys Garrett.
Apologies for the poor quality.

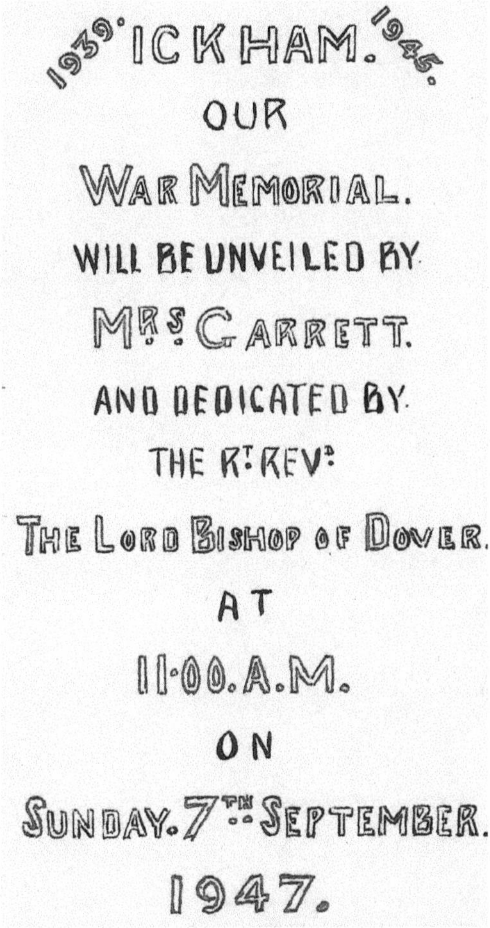

1939. ICKHAM. 1945.

OUR

WAR MEMORIAL.

WILL BE UNVEILED BY.

MRS GARRETT.

AND DEDICATED BY.

THE RT REVD

THE LORD BISHOP OF DOVER.

AT

11·00·A.M.

ON

SUNDAY. 7TH SEPTEMBER.

1947.

This is the original invitation for the official opening of
the War Memorial at Ickham church in 1947.

A grave chosen at random to commemorate Aubrey
Garrett in Suda Bay CWGC cemetery in Crete.

Major John F Bennett PWRR VR, taken just
before retirement in 2005

Acknowledgements

The help and inspiration in the production of this family history has been many years in the making, going back to the early 1980s when my mother, Gladys Bennett became more open on some of the family's history and medical problems that were encountered by some of our relatives.

My great aunt, Phoebe Newing, would tell me stories of her brothers who fought in the First World war, and how the experience changed their personalities. For years she would take me on bicycle rides to Elham and Goodnestone to see her sisters in law who used to tell me stories of their experiences during the wars.

I must give credit to the website Find my Past, certain information that had been difficult to find was held within their pages or links to the National Archives at Kew, and to Forces War records. There I could easily check orbats and battalion movements to cross reference relatives' movements. Also, I must give credit to Andrew Newson, who physically obtained the war diaries of 234 battery Heavy Anti-Aircraft from the National Archives where information was crossed referenced.

The Office for National Statistics proved a useful source of reference material as did the archive files at the National Archives. The information I have provided is accurate to the best of my knowledge and belief. Any reprints will reflect any subsequent amendments.

Thanks also to Stephen Scudder and Geoff Snell for sense checking the documents, and Fiona Doherty for the constructive criticism and David Stevenson for the confidence check. Special mention also to Sean Doherty who did magic with the black and white photographs. I must also credit James Essinger of The Conrad Press for his help, advice and mentoring.

Finally, I must thank my wife Sue, who had to put up with piles of family research material in not so neat piles around the house and the hours of bouncing ideas around, for months on end!

About the author

John Bennett was born in Canterbury and educated locally. In 1974 he joined the Royal Air Force to be trained as an Aircraft mechanic.

During the third week of basic training John together with several of his intake were asked to re-muster as firemen as they had over recruited. John decided to leave and joined the motor trade to train as a mechanic.

In 1978 he joined the Territorial Army, partly to assist in work progression and partly through curiosity as his uncle was in the TA in 1938 through to his sad death in 1941. It was through the memories of his mother and a vast number of photographs and letters that the interest in military matters was born.

In 1988 John left the motor trade and joined Sun Alliance insurance as a Staff Motor Engineer where he progressed via a convoluted route to become a team leader of motor engineers in the North of England, Scotland and Northern Ireland.

John took early retirement in 2013 and is involved with the Princess of Wales's Royal Regiment (PWRR) Regimental association, assisting with its growth and development. John is also passionate about the Regimental museum in Dover Castle and works as a volunteer assisting with outreach projects and doing talks and tours.

John is also on the Regimental Heritage Committee representing the TA and Army reserve. In addition, John is the mental Health Champion in the regimental association and is a qualified mental health first aider.